Duncan Hines®
Baking
WITH LOVE

Publications International, Ltd.

Favorite Brand Name Recipes at www.fbnr.com

Project Editor: Karen Bishea
Brand Representative: Susan Smith
Recipe development and testing: Cindy Young in The Duncan Hines Kitchens.

Photographs on pages 27, 29, 31, 35, 37, 39, 43, 45, 61, 75 by Proffitt Photography, Chicago.

Pictured on the front cover: Black Forest Torte *(page 28).*

Pictured on the back cover: Lemon Bars *(page 23).*

Microwave Cooking: Microwave ovens vary in wattage. Use the cooking times as guidelines and check for doneness before adding more time.

ISBN: 0-7853-4771-2

Manufactured in China.

8 7 6 5 4 3 2 1

CONTENTS

BUSY-DAY BROWNIES, BARS & COOKIES

PRALINE BROWNIES

BROWNIES

1 package Duncan Hines®
  Milk Chocolate Chunk
  Brownie Mix
2 eggs

⅓ cup water
⅓ cup Crisco® Vegetable
  Oil
¾ cup chopped pecans

TOPPING

¾ cup firmly packed
  brown sugar
¾ cup chopped pecans
¼ cup butter or
  margarine, melted

2 tablespoons milk
½ teaspoon vanilla extract

1 Preheat oven to 350°F. Grease bottom of 9-inch square pan.

2 **For brownies,** combine brownie mix, eggs, water, oil and ¾ cup pecans in large bowl. Stir with spoon until well blended, about 50 strokes. Spread in pan. Bake at 350°F 35 to 40 minutes. Remove from oven.

3 **For topping,** combine brown sugar, ¾ cup pecans, melted butter, milk and vanilla extract in small bowl. Stir with spoon until well blended. Spread over hot brownies. Return to oven. Bake 15 minutes or until topping is set. Cool completely. Cut into bars.   *16 brownies*

Tip: To keep leftover pecans fresh, store in freezer in airtight container.

DOUBLE "TOPPED" BROWNIES

BROWNIES

1 package Duncan Hines® Double Fudge Brownie Mix

2 eggs

⅓ cup water

¼ cup Crisco® Vegetable Oil

½ cup flaked coconut

½ cup chopped nuts

FROSTING

3 cups confectioners sugar

⅓ cup butter or margarine, softened

1½ teaspoons vanilla extract

2 to 3 tablespoons milk

TOPPING

3 squares (3 ounces) unsweetened chocolate

1 tablespoon butter or margarine

1 Preheat oven to 350°F. Grease bottom of 13×9×2-inch pan.

2 For brownies, combine brownie mix, fudge packet from Mix, eggs, water and oil in large bowl. Stir with spoon until well blended, about 50 strokes. Stir in coconut and nuts. Spread in pan. Bake at 350°F 27 to 30 minutes or until set. Cool completely.

3 For frosting, combine confectioners sugar, ⅓ cup butter and vanilla extract. Stir in milk, 1 tablespoon at a time, until frosting is of spreading consistency. Spread over brownies. Refrigerate until frosting is firm, about 30 minutes.

4 For topping, melt chocolate and 1 tablespoon butter in small bowl over hot water; stir until smooth. Drizzle over frosting. Refrigerate until chocolate is firm, about 15 minutes. Cut into bars.   *48 brownies*

Tip: Chocolate topping can be prepared in microwave oven. Place chocolate and butter in microwave-safe bowl and microwave at MEDIUM (50% power) 2 to 2½ minutes; stir until smooth.

TRIPLE CHOCOLATE COOKIES

1 package Duncan Hines® Moist Deluxe® Swiss Chocolate Cake Mix	½ cup semi-sweet chocolate chips
½ cup butter or margarine, melted	½ cup milk chocolate chips
1 egg	½ cup coarsely chopped white chocolate
	½ cup chopped pecans

1 Preheat oven to 375°F.

2 Combine cake mix, melted butter and egg in large bowl. Beat at low speed with electric mixer until blended. Stir in all 3 chocolates and pecans.

3 Drop by rounded tablespoonfuls onto ungreased baking sheets. Bake at 375°F 9 to 11 minutes. Cool 1 minute on baking sheet. Remove to cooling racks.

3½ to 4 dozen cookies

Tip: Cookies may be stored in an airtight container in freezer for up to 6 months.

BUTTERSCOTCH SPICE COOKIES

1 package Duncan Hines® Moist Deluxe® Spice Cake Mix	½ cup Crisco® Vegetable Oil
2 eggs	1 teaspoon vanilla extract
	1 cup butterscotch chips

1 Preheat oven to 375°F.

2 Combine cake mix, eggs, oil and vanilla extract in large bowl. Beat at low speed with electric mixer until blended. Stir in butterscotch chips. Drop by rounded teaspoonfuls 2 inches apart onto ungreased baking sheets. Bake at 375°F 8 to 10 minutes or until set. Cool 2 minutes on baking sheets. Remove to cooling racks. Cool completely. Store in airtight container.

3 dozen cookies

Tip: For chewy cookies, bake for 8 minutes. Cookies will be slightly puffed when removed from the oven and will settle while cooling.

EASY MINT BROWNIES

1 package Duncan Hines® Walnut Brownie Mix 4 bars (5.3 ounces each) cookies and mint chocolate candy bars	⅓ cup chopped walnuts, for garnish (optional)

1 Preheat oven to 350°F. Grease bottom of 13×9×2-inch pan.

2 Prepare and bake brownies following package directions for basic recipe chewy brownies. Break chocolate candy bars along scored lines. Place pieces immediately on hot brownies. Cover pan with aluminum foil for 3 to 5 minutes or until chocolate is shiny and soft. Spread gently to cover surface of brownies. Sprinkle with chopped walnuts, if desired. Cool completely. Cut into bars. *18 brownies*

Tip: Always use the pan size called for in Duncan Hines® recipes. Using a different size can give the brownies an altogether different texture.

CANDY BAR BROWNIES

1 package Duncan Hines® Chewy Fudge Brownie Mix (19.8 ounces) 4 bars (5.3 ounces each) milk chocolate candy bars	⅓ cup mini candy-coated milk chocolate pieces

1 Preheat oven to 350°F. Grease bottom of 13×9×2-inch pan.

2 Prepare and bake brownies following package directions for basic recipe chewy brownies. Break chocolate candy bars along scored lines. Place pieces immediately on hot brownies. Cover pan with aluminum foil for 3 to 5 minutes or until chocolate is shiny and soft. Spread gently to cover surface of brownies. Sprinkle with candy-coated chocolate pieces. Cool completely. Cut into bars. *18 brownies*

Tip: For another delicious candy topping, try sprinkling melted chocolate with ½ cup chopped chocolate-covered toffee chips.

WHITE CHOCOLATE BROWNIES

1 package Duncan Hines® Milk Chocolate Chunk Brownie Mix	⅓ cup Crisco® Vegetable Oil
2 eggs	¾ cup coarsely chopped white chocolate
⅓ cup water	¼ cup sliced almonds

1 Preheat oven to 350°F. Grease bottom of 13×9×2-inch pan.

2 Combine brownie mix, eggs, water and oil in large bowl. Stir with spoon until well blended, about 50 strokes. Stir in white chocolate. Spread in pan. Sprinkle top with almonds. Bake at 350°F 25 to 28 minutes or until set. Cool completely. Cut into bars.   *48 small or 24 large brownies*

Tip: For decadent brownies, combine 2 ounces coarsely chopped white chocolate and 2 teaspoons Crisco® Shortening in small heavy saucepan. Melt on low heat, stirring constantly. Drizzle over brownies.

CINDY'S FUDGY BROWNIES

1 package Duncan Hines® Chewy Fudge Brownie Mix (19.8 ounces)	⅓ cup Crisco® Vegetable Oil
1 egg	¾ cup semi-sweet chocolate chips
⅓ cup water	½ cup chopped pecans

1 Preheat oven to 350°F. Grease bottom of 13×9×2-inch pan.

2 Combine brownie mix, egg, water and oil in large bowl. Stir with spoon until well blended, about 50 strokes. Stir in chocolate chips. Spread in pan. Sprinkle with pecans. Bake at 350°F 25 to 28 minutes or until set. Cool completely. Cut into bars.   *24 brownies*

Tip: Overbaking brownies will cause them to become dry. Follow the recommended baking times given in recipes closely.

CHOCOLATE OAT CHEWIES

1 package Duncan Hines® Moist Deluxe® Devil's Food Cake Mix 1⅓ cups old-fashioned oats 1 cup flaked coconut, toasted and divided	¾ cup butter or margarine, melted 2 eggs, beaten 1 teaspoon vanilla extract 5 bars (1.55 ounces each) milk chocolate, cut into rectangles

1 Preheat oven to 350°F.

2 Combine cake mix, oats, ½ cup coconut, melted butter, eggs and vanilla extract in large bowl. Beat at low speed with electric mixer until blended. Cover and chill 15 minutes.

3 Shape dough into 1-inch balls. Place balls 2 inches apart on ungreased baking sheet. Bake at 350°F 12 minutes or until tops are slightly cracked. Remove from oven. Press one milk chocolate rectangle into center of each cookie. Sprinkle with remaining ½ cup coconut. Remove to cooling racks. Cool completely. Store in airtight container.   *4½ dozen cookies*

Tip: To toast coconut, spread on cookie sheet and bake at 350°F for 3 minutes. Stir and bake 1 to 2 minutes longer or until light golden brown.

 ## CHOCOLATE CHIP COOKIES

1 package Duncan Hines® Chocolate Chip Cookie Mix 1 egg	1 tablespoon water ⅓ cup MOTT'S® Natural Apple Sauce

1 Preheat oven to 375°F. Lightly grease baking sheet.

2 Follow instructions on box for MAKE DOUGH. Drop by measuring tablespoonfuls 2 inches apart onto greased baking sheets. Bake at 375°F 8 to 9 minutes. Cool 1 minute on baking sheet. Remove to cooling racks.   *4 dozen cookies*

Note: "Get it All" cookies will have a more cake-like texture than cookies made from Basic Recipe.

BUTTER FUDGE FINGERS

1 package Duncan Hines® Chewy Fudge Brownie Mix (19.8 ounces)	¼ cup semi-sweet chocolate chips
1 container Duncan Hines® Creamy Homestyle Vanilla Buttercream Frosting	½ tablespoon Crisco® Shortening

1 Preheat oven to 350°F. Grease bottom of 13×9×2-inch pan.

2 Prepare, bake and cool brownies following package directions for basic recipe chewy brownies. Spread with Buttercream frosting.

3 Place chocolate chips and shortening in small resealable plastic bag; seal. Microwave at HIGH (100% power) 30 seconds, adding 15 to 30 seconds more if needed. Knead until blended. Snip pinpoint hole in corner of bag. Drizzle chocolate over frosting. Allow chocolate to set before cutting into bars. *18 brownies*

Tip: Another method for melting the chocolate and shortening in the sealed bag is to place it in a bowl of hot water for several minutes. Dry bag with paper towel. Knead, snip and pipe as directed above.

CINNAMON CRINKLES

2 tablespoons sugar	1 teaspoon vanilla extract
½ teaspoon ground cinnamon	1 package Duncan Hines® Moist Deluxe® French Vanilla Cake Mix
2 eggs, separated	
1 teaspoon water	48 whole almonds or pecan halves, for garnish
¾ cup butter or margarine, softened	

1 Preheat oven to 375°F. Combine sugar and cinnamon in small bowl. Set aside. Combine egg whites and water in another small bowl; beat lightly with fork. Set aside.

2 Combine butter, egg yolks and vanilla extract in large bowl. Blend in cake mix gradually. Beat at low speed with electric mixer until blended. Roll 1 rounded teaspoon of dough into ball. Dip half the ball into egg white mixture then into cinnamon-sugar mixture. Place ball sugar side up on ungreased baking sheet. Press nut on top. Repeat with remaining dough, placing balls 2 inches apart.

3 Bake at 375°F 9 to 12 minutes or until edges are light golden brown. Cool 2 minutes on baking sheets. Remove to cooling racks. Store in airtight container. *48 cookies*

Tip: Cookies will be slightly puffed when removed from the oven and will settle during cooling.

TOFFEE CRUNCH FANTASY

1 package Duncan Hines® Dark 'n Chunky Brownie Mix	2½ cups frozen non-dairy whipped topping, thawed
2 eggs	⅔ cup toffee chips, divided (see Tip)
⅓ cup water	
⅓ cup Crisco® Vegetable Oil	

1 Preheat oven to 350°F. Grease bottom of 9-inch round cake pan.

2 Combine brownie mix, eggs, water and oil in large bowl. Stir with spoon until well blended, about 50 strokes. Spread in pan. Bake at 350°F 35 to 40 minutes or until set. Cool completely.

3 Combine whipped topping and ½ cup toffee chips in large bowl. Spread on top of brownies. Garnish with remaining toffee chips. Refrigerate until ready to serve. Cut into wedges. *12 to 16 servings*

Tip: Coarsely chop several chocolate-covered toffee candy bars to prepare toffee chips, if ready-made toffee chips are not available.

CANDY DANDY BROWNIES

BROWNIES

1 package Duncan Hines® Chewy Fudge Brownie Mix (19.8 ounces)

1 egg
⅓ cup water
⅓ cup Crisco® Vegetable Oil

TOPPING

⅓ cup sugar
⅓ cup light corn syrup

⅓ cup Jif® Creamy Peanut Butter

FROSTING

½ cup semi-sweet chocolate chips
2 tablespoons butter or margarine

1 tablespoon light corn syrup
¼ cup sliced almonds, for garnish

1 Preheat oven to 350°F. Grease bottom of 13×9×2-inch pan.

2 **For brownies,** combine brownie mix, egg, water and oil in large bowl. Stir with spoon until well blended, about 50 strokes. Spread in pan. Bake at 350°F 25 to 28 minutes or until set. Cool in pan while preparing topping.

3 **For topping,** combine sugar and ⅓ cup corn syrup in heavy saucepan. Bring to boil on medium heat. Stir in peanut butter. Spread over warm brownies. Cool 10 to 15 minutes.

4 **For frosting,** combine chocolate chips, butter and 1 tablespoon corn syrup in pan. Cook, stirring constantly, on low heat until melted. Spread frosting over peanut butter layer. Sprinkle with almonds. Cool completely. Refrigerate until chocolate is firm, about 15 minutes. Cut into bars.   *24 bars*

Tip: Always mix brownies by hand. Never use an electric mixer.

RICH 'N' CREAMY BROWNIE BARS

BROWNIES

1 package Duncan Hines®
Double Fudge
Brownie Mix

2 eggs

⅓ cup water
¼ cup Crisco® Vegetable
Oil
½ cup chopped pecans

TOPPING

1 package (8 ounces)
cream cheese,
softened

2 eggs

1 pound (3½ cups)
confectioners sugar
1 teaspoon vanilla extract

1 Preheat oven to 350°F. Grease bottom of 13×9×2-inch pan.

2 **For brownies,** combine brownie mix, fudge packet from Mix, 2 eggs, water and oil in large bowl. Stir with spoon until well blended, about 50 strokes. Stir in pecans. Spread evenly in pan.

3 **For topping,** beat cream cheese in large bowl at medium speed with electric mixer until smooth. Beat in 2 eggs, confectioners sugar and vanilla extract until smooth. Spread evenly over brownie mixture. Bake at 350°F 45 to 50 minutes or until edges and top are golden brown and shiny. Cool completely. Refrigerate until well chilled. Cut into bars.

48 bars

Tip: To soften cream cheese quickly, unwrap and place in microwave-safe bowl. Microwave at HIGH (100% power) 15 seconds; add 10 to 15 seconds, if needed.

DOUBLE CHOCOLATE CHEWIES

1 package Duncan Hines® Moist Deluxe® Butter Recipe Fudge Cake Mix	1 package (6 ounces) semi-sweet chocolate chips
2 eggs	1 cup chopped nuts
½ cup butter or margarine, melted	Confectioners sugar (optional)

1 Preheat oven to 350°F. Grease 13×9×2-inch pan.

2 Combine cake mix, eggs and melted butter in large bowl. Stir until thoroughly blended. (Mixture will be stiff.) Stir in chocolate chips and nuts. Press mixture evenly into greased pan. Bake at 350°F 25 to 30 minutes or until toothpick inserted in center comes out clean. DO NOT OVERBAKE. Cool completely. Cut into bars. Dust with confectioners sugar, if desired.   *36 bars*

Tip: For a special effect, cut paper towel into ¼-inch wide strips. Place strips in diagonal pattern on top of cooled bars before cutting. Place confectioners sugar in small strainer. Tap strainer lightly to dust surface with sugar. Carefully remove strips.

TOFFEE BROWNIE BARS

CRUST

¾ cup butter or margarine, softened	1 egg yolk
¾ cup firmly packed brown sugar	¾ teaspoon vanilla extract
	1½ cups all-purpose flour

FILLING

1 package Duncan Hines® Chewy Fudge Brownie Mix (19.8 ounces)	⅓ cup water
1 egg	⅓ cup Crisco® Vegetable Oil

TOPPING

1 package (12 ounces) milk chocolate chips, melted	¾ cup finely chopped pecans

1 Preheat oven to 350°F. Grease 15½×10½×1-inch pan.

2 **For crust,** combine butter, brown sugar, egg yolk and vanilla extract in large bowl. Stir in flour. Spread in pan. Bake 15 minutes or until golden.

3 **For filling,** prepare brownie mix following package directions. Spread over hot crust. Bake 15 minutes or until surface appears set. Cool 30 minutes.

4 **For topping,** spread melted chocolate on top of brownie layer; sprinkle with pecans. Cool completely.   *48 bars*

Tip: Bars may be made ahead and frozen in an airtight container for several weeks.

LEMON BARS

1 package Duncan Hines® Moist Deluxe® Lemon Supreme Cake Mix	¼ cup lemon juice
3 eggs, divided	2 teaspoons grated lemon peel
⅓ cup butter-flavor shortening	½ teaspoon baking powder
½ cup granulated sugar	¼ teaspoon salt
	Confectioners sugar

1 Preheat oven to 350°F.

2 Combine cake mix, 1 egg and shortening in large mixing bowl. Beat at low speed with electric mixer until crumbs form. Reserve 1 cup. Pat remaining mixture lightly into ungreased 13×9-inch pan. Bake 15 minutes or until lightly browned.

3 Combine remaining 2 eggs, granulated sugar, lemon juice, lemon peel, baking powder and salt in medium mixing bowl. Beat at medium speed with electric mixer until light and foamy. Pour over hot crust. Sprinkle with reserved crumb mixture. Bake 15 minutes or until lightly browned. Sprinkle with confectioners sugar. Cool in pan. Cut into bars.

30 to 32 bars

Tip: These bars are also delicious using DUNCAN HINES® Moist Deluxe® Yellow Cake Mix.

COCONUT CLOUDS

2⅔ cups flaked coconut, divided	½ cup Crisco® Vegetable Oil
1 package Duncan Hines® Moist Deluxe® Yellow Cake Mix	¼ cup water
	1 teaspoon almond extract
1 egg	

1 Preheat oven to 350°F. Place 1⅓ cups coconut in medium bowl; set aside.

2 Combine cake mix, egg, oil, water and almond extract in large bowl. Beat at low speed with electric mixer. Stir in remaining 1⅓ cups reserved coconut. Drop rounded teaspoonful dough into reserved coconut. Roll to cover lightly. Place on ungreased baking sheet. Repeat with remaining dough, placing balls 2 inches apart. Bake at 350°F 10 to 12 minutes or until light golden brown. Cool 1 minute on baking sheets. Remove to cooling racks. Cool completely. Store in airtight container.   *3½ dozen cookies*

Tip: To save time when forming dough into balls, use a 1-inch spring-operated cookie scoop. Spring-operated cookie scoops are available at kitchen specialty shops.

CHEWY FUDGE BROWNIES

1 package Duncan Hines® Chewy Fudge Brownie Mix (19.8 ounces)	1 egg
	1 tablespoon water
	⅓ cup MOTT'S® Natural Apple Sauce

1 Preheat oven to 350°F. Lightly grease 13×9-inch pan.

2 Follow instructions on box for PREPARE and MAKE BATTER. Spread batter in pan. Bake at 350°F 23 to 26 minutes or until set. Cool completely.   *20 brownies*

Tip: If using a 9×9-inch pan, bake brownies 33 to 36 minutes; if using an 8×8-inch pan, bake brownies 34 to 37 minutes.

BEAT THE CLOCK CAKES

STRAWBERRY VANILLA CAKE

1 package Duncan Hines® Moist Deluxe® French Vanilla Cake Mix
1 container Duncan Hines® Creamy Homestyle Vanilla Buttercream Frosting, divided

⅓ cup seedless strawberry jam
Fresh strawberries, for garnish (optional)

1 Preheat oven to 350°F. Grease and flour two 8- or 9-inch round pans.

2 Prepare, bake and cool cakes following package directions for basic recipe.

3 To assemble, place one cake layer on serving plate. Place ¼ cup Vanilla frosting in small resealable plastic bag. Snip off one corner. Pipe a bead of frosting on top of layer around outer edge. Fill remaining area with strawberry jam. Top with second cake layer. Spread remaining frosting on sides and top of cake. Decorate with fresh strawberries, if desired.

12 to 16 servings

Tip: You may substitute Duncan Hines® Vanilla or Cream Cheese frosting for the Vanilla Buttercream frosting, if desired.

CHOCOLATE SPRINKLE ANGEL FOOD CAKE

1 package Duncan Hines® Angel Food Cake Mix	3 tablespoons chocolate sprinkles

1 Remove top rack from oven; move remaining rack to lowest position. Preheat oven to 350°F.

2 Prepare batter following package directions. Fold in chocolate sprinkles. Pour batter into ungreased 10-inch tube pan. Bake and cool following package directions.

12 to 16 servings

Tip: For a quick finish, simply dust cake with confectioners sugar.

BLACK FOREST TORTE

1 package Duncan Hines® Moist Deluxe® Dark Chocolate Fudge Cake Mix 2½ cups whipping cream, chilled	2½ tablespoons confectioners sugar 1 (21-ounce) can cherry pie filling

1 Preheat oven to 350°F. Grease and flour two 9-inch round cake pans.

2 Prepare, bake and cool cake as directed on package.

3 Beat whipping cream in large bowl until soft peaks form. Add sugar gradually. Beat until stiff peaks form.

4 To assemble, place one cake layer on serving plate. Spread two-thirds cherry pie filling on cake to within ½ inch of edge. Spread 1½ cups whipped cream mixture over cherry pie filling. Top with second cake layer. Frost sides and top with remaining whipped cream mixture. Spread remaining cherry pie filling on top to within 1 inch of edge. Refrigerate until ready to serve.

12 to 16 servings

Tip: Chill the cherry pie filling for easy spreading on cake. Also, garnish the cake with grated semisweet chocolate or white chocolate curls.

SIMPLE BOSTON CREAM PIES

1 package Duncan Hines® Moist Deluxe® Yellow Cake Mix 4 containers (3½ ounces each) ready-to-eat vanilla pudding	1 container Duncan Hines® Creamy Homestyle Chocolate Frosting

1 Preheat oven to 350°F. Grease and flour two 8- or 9-inch round pans.

2 Prepare, bake and cool cake following package directions for basic recipe.

3 To assemble, place each cake layer on serving plate. Split layers in half horizontally. Spread contents of 2 containers of vanilla pudding on bottom layer of one cake. Place top layer on filling. Repeat for second cake layer. Remove lid and foil top of Chocolate frosting container. Heat in microwave oven at HIGH (100% power) 25 to 30 seconds. Stir. (Mixture should be thin.) Spread half the chocolate glaze over top of each cake. Refrigerate until ready to serve.

12 to 16 servings

Tip: For a richer flavor, substitute Duncan Hines® Butter Recipe Golden cake mix in place of Yellow cake mix.

CHOCOLATE MARBLE ANGEL FOOD CAKE

1 package Duncan Hines® Angel Food Cake Mix	3 tablespoons chocolate syrup

1 Remove top rack from oven; move remaining rack to lowest position. Preheat oven to 350°F.

2 Prepare batter following package directions for basic recipe. Remove half the batter to another bowl; set aside. Add chocolate syrup to batter. Fold gently until blended. Alternate large spoonfuls of white and chocolate batters in ungreased 10-inch tube pan. Bake and cool following package directions.

12 to 16 servings

Tip: Serve slices drizzled with chocolate syrup for extra chocolate flavor.

DOUBLE FUDGE MARBLE CAKE

1 package Duncan Hines®
    Moist Deluxe® Fudge
    Marble Cake Mix
1 container Duncan
    Hines® Creamy
    Homestyle Milk
    Chocolate Frosting

¼ cup hot fudge topping

1 Preheat oven to 350°F. Grease and flour 13×9×2-inch pan.

2 Prepare, bake and cool cake following package directions for basic recipe.

3 Frost top of cooled cake with Milk Chocolate frosting. Place hot fudge topping in small microwave-safe bowl. Microwave at HIGH (100% power) 30 seconds or until thin. Drop hot fudge by spoonfuls on top of cake in 18 places. Pull tip of knife once through each hot fudge dollop to form heart shapes.   *12 to 16 servings*

Tip: Hot fudge topping may also be marbled in frosting by using flat blade of knife to swirl slightly.

CREAMY SWISS POUND CAKE

CAKE

1 package Duncan Hines®
    Moist Deluxe® Swiss
    Chocolate Cake Mix
1 package (4-serving size)
    chocolate instant
    pudding and pie
    filling mix

4 eggs
1¼ cups milk
½ cup Crisco® Vegetable
    Oil
1 cup mini semi-sweet
    chocolate chips

TOPPING

1 cup whipping cream
¼ cup granulated sugar
½ teaspoon vanilla extract
    Fresh raspberries, for
    garnish (optional)

Mini semi-sweet
    chocolate chips, for
    garnish (optional)

1 Preheat oven to 350°F. Grease and flour 10-inch Bundt® or tube pan.

2 **For cake,** combine cake mix, pudding mix, eggs, milk and oil in large bowl. Beat at low speed with electric mixer until moistened. Beat at medium speed 2 minutes. Stir in 1 cup chocolate chips. Pour into pan. Bake at 350°F 50 to 60 minutes or until toothpick inserted in center comes out clean. Cool in pan 25 minutes. Invert onto cooling rack. Cool completely.

3 **For topping,** place whipping cream, sugar and vanilla in medium bowl. Beat at high speed with electric mixer until stiff peaks form. Spoon whipped cream mixture on top of cooled cake. Garnish with fresh raspberries and chocolate chips, if desired. Refrigerate leftovers.   *12 to 16 servings*

COUNTRY OVEN CARROT CAKE

1 package Duncan Hines® Moist Deluxe® Yellow Cake Mix	2 teaspoons ground cinnamon
4 eggs	1 container Duncan Hines® Creamy Homestyle Cream Cheese Frosting
3 cups grated carrots	
1 cup finely chopped nuts	
½ cup Crisco® Vegetable Oil	

1 Preheat oven to 350°F. Grease and flour 13×9×2-inch pan (see Tip).

2 Combine cake mix, eggs, carrots, nuts, oil and cinnamon in large bowl. Beat at low speed with electric mixer until moistened. Beat at medium speed 2 minutes. Pour into pan. Bake at 350°F 40 to 45 minutes or until toothpick inserted in center comes out clean. Cool completely. Frost cake with Cream Cheese frosting.   *12 to 16 servings*

Tip: Carrot cake can also be baked in two 8- or 9-inch round cake pans at 350°F 35 to 40 minutes or until toothpick inserted in center comes out clean. Cool cakes following package directions. Fill and frost cooled cakes. Garnish with whole pecans.

CHOCOLATE BANANA CAKE

CAKE

1 package Duncan Hines®
Moist Deluxe® Devil's
Food Cake Mix
3 eggs

1⅓ cups milk
½ cup Crisco® Vegetable
Oil

TOPPING

1 package (4-serving size)
banana cream instant
pudding and pie
filling mix
1 cup milk

1 cup whipping cream,
whipped
1 medium banana
Lemon juice
Chocolate sprinkles

1 Preheat oven to 350°F. Grease and flour 13×9×2-inch pan.

2 **For cake,** combine cake mix, eggs, milk and oil in large bowl. Beat at low speed with electric mixer until moistened. Beat at medium speed 2 minutes. Pour into pan. Bake at 350°F 35 to 38 minutes or until toothpick inserted in center comes out clean. Cool completely.

3 **For topping,** combine pudding mix and milk in large bowl. Stir until smooth. Fold in whipped cream. Spread on top of cooled cake. Slice banana; dip in lemon juice, arrange on top. Garnish with chocolate sprinkles. Refrigerate until ready to serve. *12 to 16 servings*

Tip: A wire whisk is a great utensil to use when making instant pudding. It quickly eliminates all lumps.

EASY CREAM CAKE

1 package Duncan Hines®
    Moist Deluxe® White
    Cake Mix
3 egg whites
1⅓ cups half-and-half
2 tablespoons Crisco®
    Vegetable Oil
1 cup flaked coconut,
    finely chopped
½ cup finely chopped
    pecans
2 containers Duncan
    Hines® Creamy
    Homestyle Cream
    Cheese Frosting

1 Preheat oven to 350°F. Grease and flour three 8-inch round pans.

2 Combine cake mix, egg whites, half-and-half, oil, coconut and pecans in large bowl. Beat at low speed with electric mixer until moistened. Beat at medium speed 2 minutes. Pour into pans. Bake at 350°F 22 to 25 minutes or until toothpick inserted in center comes out clean. Cool following package directions.

3 To assemble, place one cake layer on serving plate. Spread with ¾ cup Cream Cheese frosting. Place second cake layer on top. Spread with ¾ cup frosting. Top with third layer. Spread ¾ cup frosting on top only.   *12 to 16 servings*

Tip: Spread leftover frosting between graham crackers for an easy snack.

STRAWBERRY STRIPE REFRIGERATOR CAKE

CAKE

1 package Duncan Hines® Moist Deluxe® White Cake Mix

2 packages (10 ounces) frozen sweetened strawberry slices, thawed

TOPPING

1 package (4-serving) vanilla instant pudding and pie filling mix
1 cup milk

1 cup whipping cream, whipped
Fresh strawberries, for garnish (optional)

1 Preheat oven to 350°F. Grease and flour 13×9×2-inch pan.

2 **For cake,** prepare, bake and cool following package directions. Poke holes 1 inch apart in top of cake using handle of wooden spoon. Puree thawed strawberries with juice in blender or food processor. Spoon evenly over top of cake, allowing mixture to soak into holes.

3 **For topping,** combine pudding mix and milk in large bowl. Stir until smooth. Fold in whipped cream. Spread over cake. Decorate with fresh strawberries, if desired. Refrigerate at least 4 hours.   *12 to 16 servings*

Tip: For a Neapolitan Refrigerator Cake, replace the White Cake Mix with Duncan Hines® Moist Deluxe® Devil's Food Cake Mix and follow directions listed above.

REFRESHING LEMON CAKE

1 package Duncan Hines® Moist Deluxe® Butter Recipe Golden Cake Mix 1 container Duncan Hines® Creamy Homestyle Cream Cheese Frosting	¾ cup purchased lemon curd Lemon drop candies, crushed, for garnish (optional)

1 Preheat oven to 375°F. Grease and flour two 8- or 9-inch round cake pans.

2 Prepare, bake and cool cake following package directions for basic recipe.

3 To assemble, place one cake layer on serving plate. Place ¼ cup Cream Cheese frosting in small resealable plastic bag. Snip off one corner. Pipe a bead of frosting on top of layer around outer edge. Fill remaining area with lemon curd. Top with second cake layer. Spread remaining frosting on sides and top of cake. Garnish top of cake with crushed lemon candies, if desired.   *12 to 16 servings*

Tip: You may substitute Duncan Hines® Vanilla or Vanilla Buttercream frosting for the Cream Cheese frosting, if desired.

Marbled Cake Instructions

How to marble any two Duncan Hines® Cake Mixes

Now you can make delightfully creative marbled cakes with Duncan Hines®! Our cake specialists have put together all the information you'll need to make beautiful marbled cakes. You'll find a helpful chart detailing which flavors look and taste great together, along with mixing, measuring and baking instructions. Marbled cake requires 2 different cake mixes, one mix as the base mix and the other as the marbling mix. These instructions yield 2 baked cakes. For example, you will have enough batter to prepare one 13×9-inch cake and one Bundt® cake. Freeze one cake to enjoy at a later date, if desired.

Part A: Basic Instructions

Choose one mix flavor you will use as the base and one mix flavor you will marble into the base flavor. See Part C for the recommended flavor combination chart.

1 PREPARE
Preheat oven to 350°F. Grease and flour pan(s).

2 ADD (for each box of mix)

White Cake	Yellow Cake	Chocolate Cake
1⅓ cups water 3 egg whites 2 tablespoons oil	1⅓ cups water 3 eggs ⅓ cup oil	1⅓ cups water 3 eggs ½ cup oil
Yield = 5 cups batter	Yield = 5 cups batter	Yield = 5 cups batter

3 MIX

Blend at low speed until moistened. Mix 2 minutes at medium speed, scraping bottom and sides of bowl with spatula for uniform batter.

Pour base flavor batter into pan following chart in Part B. Spoon marble flavor cake batter onto base flavor batter in pan. Swirl with knife.

4 BAKE

See Part B for bake times. Use the chart that matches your base mix flavor.

5 COOL

Cool 15 minutes in pan(s) on wire rack. For Bundt® or tube pan, cool 25 minutes. Remove from pan(s) and cool completely before frosting.

Part B: Batter Amount and Bake Time Charts

Bake Chart for Yellow Base Flavor Marbled Cakes

Use this chart for Duncan Hines® Moist Deluxe® French Vanilla, Lemon Supreme, Orange Supreme, Banana Supreme, Spice, Pineapple Supreme, Strawberry Supreme and Caramel Cake Mixes.

Pan Size	Base Flavor Cups of Batter	Marble Flavor Cups of Batter	Total Cups of batter per pan	Bake Time (minutes)
Two 8-inch round	2	½	2½	33–36
Two 9-inch round	2	½	2½	28–31
13×9×2-inch rectangular	4	1	5	32–35
Bundt® or tube pan	4	1	5	38–43

Bake Chart for Chocolate Base Flavor Marbled Cakes

Use this chart for Duncan Hines® Moist Deluxe® Devil's Food, Swiss, Dark Chocolate Fudge and Chocolate Mocha Cake Mixes.

Pan Size	Base Flavor Cups of Batter	Marble Flavor Cups of Batter	Total Cups of batter per pan	Bake Time (minutes)
Two 8-inch round	2	½	2½	35–38
Two 9-inch round	2	½	2½	30–33
13×9×2-inch rectangular	4	1	5	35–38
Bundt® or tube pan	4	1	5	45–50

Bake Chart for White Base Flavor Marbled Cakes

Use this chart for Duncan Hines® Moist Deluxe® White Cake Mix.

Pan Size	Base Flavor Cups of Batter	Marble Flavor Cups of Batter	Total Cups of batter per pan	Bake Time (minutes)
Two 8-inch round	2	½	2½	32–35
Two 9-inch round	2	½	2½	28–31
13×9×2-inch rectangular	4	1	5	32–35
Bundt® or tube pan	4	1	5	43–48

Part C: Flavor Combination Chart

Recommendations for base and marbling flavors using Duncan Hines® Moist Deluxe® Cake Mixes

BASE FLAVORS	MARBLING FLAVORS	White	French Vanilla	Strawberry	Lemon	Peach	Orange	Pineapple	Banana	Caramel	Devil's Food	Swiss Chocolate	Dark Chocolate Fudge	Chocolate Mocha
White				X	X	X	X	X	X	X	X	X	X	X
French Vanilla				X					X	X	X	X	X	X
Strawberry		X	X								X	X	X	X
Lemon		X	X											
Peach		X	X											
Orange		X	X											
Pineapple		X	X											
Banana		X	X											
Caramel		X	X								X	X	X	X
Devil's Food		X	X	X					X	X				
Swiss Chocolate		X	X	X					X	X				
Dark Chocolate Fudge		X	X	X					X	X				
Spice		X	X											
Chocolate Mocha		X	X	X						X				

Note: This does not include Angel Food or Butter Recipe Cake Mixes

EASIEST-EVER MUFFINS & QUICK BREADS

BERRY FILLED MUFFINS

1 package Duncan Hines® Blueberry Muffin Mix	¼ cup strawberry jam
1 egg	2 tablespoons sliced almonds
½ cup water	

1 Preheat oven to 400°F. Place 2½-inch paper or foil liners in 8 muffin cups.

2 Rinse blueberries from Mix with cold water and drain.

3 Empty muffin mix into bowl. Break up any lumps. Add egg and water. Stir until moistened, about 50 strokes. Fill cups half full with batter.

4 Fold blueberries into strawberry jam. Spoon on top of batter in each cup. Spread gently. Cover with remaining batter. Sprinkle with almonds. Bake at 400°F 17 to 20 minutes or until set and golden brown. Cool in pan 5 to 10 minutes. Carefully loosen muffins from pan. Remove to cooling racks. Serve warm or cool completely. *8 muffins*

Tip: For a delicious flavor variation, try using blackberry or red raspberry jam.

ORANGE CINNAMON SWIRL BREAD

BREAD
1 package Duncan Hines®
   Cinnamon Swirl
   Muffin Mix
1 egg

⅔ cup orange juice
1 tablespoon grated
   orange peel

ORANGE GLAZE
½ cup confectioners sugar
2 to 3 teaspoons orange
   juice
1 teaspoon grated orange
   peel

Quartered orange slices,
   for garnish (optional)

1 Preheat oven to 350°F. Grease and flour 8½×4½×2½-inch loaf pan.

2 **For bread,** combine muffin mix and contents of topping packet from Mix in large bowl. Break up any lumps. Add egg, ⅔ cup orange juice and 1 tablespoon orange peel. Stir until moistened, about 50 strokes. Knead swirl packet from Mix for 10 seconds before opening. Squeeze contents on top of batter. Swirl into batter with knife or spatula, folding from bottom of bowl to get an even swirl. DO NOT COMPLETELY MIX IN. Pour into pan. Bake at 350°F 55 to 60 minutes or until toothpick inserted in center comes out clean. Cool in pan 10 minutes. Loosen loaf from pan. Invert onto cooling rack. Turn right side up. Cool completely.

3 **For orange glaze,** place confectioners sugar in small bowl. Add orange juice, 1 teaspoon at a time, stirring until smooth and desired consistency. Stir in 1 teaspoon orange peel. Drizzle over loaf. Garnish with orange slices, if desired.

1 loaf (12 slices)

Tip: If glaze becomes too thin, add more confectioners sugar. If glaze is too thick, add more orange juice.

LEMON BLUEBERRY LOAF

BREAD

1 package Duncan Hines® Blueberry Muffin Mix	½ cup milk
1 egg	1 tablespoon grated lemon peel
½ cup dairy sour cream	½ cup chopped pecans

GLAZE

⅓ cup granulated sugar	2 tablespoons lemon juice

1 Preheat oven to 350°F. Grease and flour 9×5-inch loaf pan.

2 Rinse blueberries from Mix with cold water and drain.

3 **For bread,** empty muffin mix into medium bowl. Break up any lumps. Add egg, sour cream, milk and grated lemon peel. Stir until moistened, about 50 strokes. Fold in blueberries and pecans. Pour into pan. Bake at 350°F 60 to 65 minutes or until toothpick inserted in center comes out clean. Poke holes in top of warm loaf with toothpick or long-tined fork.

4 **For glaze,** combine sugar and lemon juice in small saucepan. Cook on medium heat, stirring constantly, until sugar dissolves. Spoon hot glaze evenly over loaf. Cool in pan 15 minutes. Loosen loaf from pan. Invert onto cooling rack. Turn right side up. Cool completely. *1 loaf (12 slices)*

Tip: When grating lemon peel, avoid the bitter white portion known as the pith.

CARAMEL PECAN SPICE CAKES

1 package Duncan Hines® Moist Deluxe® Spice Cake Mix	⅓ cup Crisco® Vegetable Oil
1 package (4-serving size) vanilla instant pudding and pie filling mix	1½ cups pecan pieces, toasted and finely chopped (see Tip)
4 eggs	1 container Duncan Hines® Creamy Homestyle Caramel Frosting
1 cup water	

1 Preheat oven to 350°F. Grease and flour two 8½×4½×2½-inch loaf pans.

2 Combine cake mix, pudding mix, eggs, water and oil in large bowl. Beat at low speed with electric mixer until moistened. Beat at medium speed 2 minutes. Stir in toasted pecans. Pour batter into pans. Bake at 350°F 55 to 60 minutes or until toothpick inserted in center comes out clean. Cool in pans 15 minutes. Loosen loaves from pans. Invert onto cooling rack. Turn right sides up. Cool completely.

3 Spread Caramel frosting evenly on cooled loaves. Garnish with pecan halves and maraschino cherry halves before glaze sets. *2 loaves (24 slices)*

Tip: To toast pecans, spread pecan pieces evenly on baking sheet. Toast in 350°F oven about 8 minutes or until fragrant. Cool completely.

BLUEBERRY ORANGE MUFFINS

1 package Duncan Hines® Blueberry Muffin Mix	½ cup orange juice
2 egg whites	1 teaspoon grated orange peel

1 Preheat oven to 400°F. Grease 2½-inch muffin cups (or use paper liners).

2 Rinse blueberries from Mix with cold water and drain.

3 Empty muffin mix into large bowl. Break up any lumps. Add egg whites, orange juice and orange peel. Stir until moistened, about 50 strokes. Fold blueberries gently into batter.

4 For large muffins, fill cups two-thirds full. Bake at 400°F 18 to 21 minutes or until toothpick inserted in center comes out clean. (For medium muffins, fill cups half full. Bake at 400°F 16 to 19 minutes or until toothpick inserted in center comes out clean.) Cool in pan 5 to 10 minutes. Carefully loosen muffins from pan. Remove to cooling racks. Serve warm or cool completely. *8 large or 12 medium muffins*

Tip: Freeze extra grated orange peel for future use.

CRANBERRY PECAN MUFFINS

1½ cups fresh or frozen cranberries	1 egg
¼ cup light corn syrup	¾ cup water or milk
1 package Duncan Hines® Cinnamon Swirl Muffin Mix	½ cup chopped pecans

1 Preheat oven to 400°F. Place 14 (2½-inch) paper liners in muffin cups (see Tip). Place cranberries and corn syrup in heavy saucepan. Cook on medium heat, stirring occasionally, until cranberries pop and mixture is slightly thickened. Drain cranberries in small strainer; set aside.

2 Empty muffin mix into medium bowl. Break up any lumps. Add egg and water. Stir until moistened, about 50 strokes. Stir in cranberries and pecans. Knead swirl packet from Mix for 10 seconds before opening. Cut off 1 end of swirl packet. Squeeze contents over top of batter. Swirl into batter with knife or spatula. DO NOT COMPLETELY MIX IN. Spoon batter into muffin cups (see Tip). Sprinkle with contents of topping packet from Mix. Bake at 400°F 18 to 22 minutes or until toothpick inserted in center comes out clean. Cool in pans 5 to 10 minutes. Remove to cooling racks. Serve warm or cool completely. *14 muffins*

Tip: Fill an equal number of muffin cups in each muffin pan with batter. For more even baking, fill empty muffin cups with ½ inch of water.

SOCK-IT-TO-ME CAKE

STREUSEL FILLING
1 package Duncan Hines®
    Moist Deluxe® Butter
    Recipe Golden Cake
    Mix, divided
2 tablespoons brown
    sugar

2 teaspoons ground
    cinnamon
1 cup finely chopped
    pecans

CAKE
4 eggs
1 cup dairy sour cream
⅓ cup Crisco® Vegetable
    Oil

¼ cup water
¼ cup granulated sugar

GLAZE
1 cup confectioners sugar

1 or 2 tablespoons milk

1 Preheat oven to 375°F. Grease and flour 10-inch tube pan.

2 **For streusel filling,** combine 2 tablespoons cake mix, brown sugar and cinnamon in medium bowl. Stir in pecans. Set aside.

3 **For cake,** combine remaining cake mix, eggs, sour cream, oil, water and granulated sugar in large bowl. Beat at medium speed with electric mixer 2 minutes. Pour two-thirds of batter into pan. Sprinkle with streusel filling. Spoon remaining batter evenly over filling. Bake at 375°F 45 to 55 minutes or until toothpick inserted in center comes out clean. Cool in pan 25 minutes. Invert onto serving plate. Cool completely.

4 **For glaze,** combine confectioners sugar and milk in small bowl. Stir until smooth. Drizzle over cake.

12 to 16 servings

Tip: For a quick glaze, place ½ cup Duncan Hines® Creamy Homestyle Vanilla Frosting in small microwave-safe bowl. Microwave at HIGH (100% power) 10 seconds; add 5 to 10 seconds, if needed. Stir until smooth and thin.

SPRING BREAK BLUEBERRY COFFEECAKE

TOPPING

½ cup flaked coconut
¼ cup firmly packed
    brown sugar
2 tablespoons butter or
    margarine, softened

1 tablespoon all-purpose
    flour

CAKE

1 package Duncan Hines®
    Blueberry Muffin Mix
1 can (8 ounces) crushed
    pineapple with juice,
    undrained

1 egg
¼ cup water

1 Preheat oven to 350°F. Grease 9-inch square pan.

2 **For topping,** combine coconut, brown sugar, butter and flour in small bowl. Mix with fork until well blended. Set aside.

3 Rinse blueberries from Mix with cold water and drain.

4 **For cake,** empty muffin mix into medium bowl. Break up any lumps. Add pineapple with juice, egg and water. Stir until moistened, about 50 strokes. Fold in blueberries. Spread in pan. Sprinkle reserved topping over batter. Bake at 350°F 30 to 35 minutes or until toothpick inserted in center comes out clean. Serve warm or cool completely.   *9 servings*

Tip: To keep blueberries from discoloring batter, drain on paper towels after rinsing.

COCONUT CHOCOLATE CHIP LOAF

1 package Duncan Hines® Chocolate Chip Muffin Mix	1 egg
1⅓ cups toasted flaked coconut (see Tip)	¾ cup water
	½ teaspoon vanilla extract
	Confectioners sugar, for garnish (optional)

1 Preheat oven to 350°F. Grease and flour 9×5×3-inch loaf pan.

2 Empty muffin mix into medium bowl. Break up any lumps. Add coconut, egg, water and vanilla extract. Stir until moistened, about 50 strokes. Pour into pan. Bake at 350°F 45 to 50 minutes or until toothpick inserted in center comes out clean. Cool in pan 15 minutes. Invert onto cooling rack. Turn right side up. Cool completely. Dust with confectioners sugar, if desired.   *1 loaf (12 slices)*

Tip: Spread coconut evenly on baking sheet. Toast at 350°F 5 minutes. Stir and toast 1 to 2 minutes longer or until light golden brown.

KIDS CAN-DO!

BANANA SPLIT CAKE

1 package Duncan Hines® Moist Deluxe® Banana Supreme Cake Mix	2 to 3 bananas
3 eggs	1 can (16 ounces) chocolate syrup
1⅓ cups water	1 container (8 ounces) frozen whipped topping, thawed
½ cup all-purpose flour	½ cup chopped walnuts
⅓ cup Crisco® Vegetable Oil	Colored sprinkles
1 cup semi-sweet mini chocolate chips	Maraschino cherries with stems, for garnish

1 Preheat oven to 350°F. Grease and flour 13×9×2-inch pan.

2 Combine cake mix, eggs, water, flour and oil in large bowl. Beat at low speed with electric mixer until moistened. Beat at medium speed 2 minutes. Stir in chocolate chips. Pour into pan. Bake at 350°F 32 to 35 minutes or until toothpick inserted in center comes out clean. Cool completely.

3 Slice bananas. Cut cake into squares; top with banana slices. Drizzle with chocolate syrup. Top with whipped topping, walnuts and sprinkles. Garnish with maraschino cherries.   *12 to 16 servings*

Tip: Dip bananas in diluted lemon juice to prevent darkening.

ICE CREAM CONE CAKES

1 package Duncan Hines®
   Moist Deluxe® Cake
   Mix (any flavor)
1 container Duncan
   Hines® Creamy
   Homestyle Chocolate
   Frosting
1 container Duncan
   Hines® Creamy
   Homestyle Vanilla
   Frosting

Chocolate sprinkles
Assorted decors
Jelly beans
2 maraschino cherries, for
   garnish

1 Preheat oven to 350°F. Grease and flour one 8-inch round cake pan and one 8-inch square pan.

2 Prepare cake following package directions for basic recipe. Pour about 2 cups batter into round pan. Pour about 3 cups batter into square pan. Bake at 350°F 30 to 35 minutes or until toothpick inserted in center comes out clean. Cool following package directions.

3 To assemble, cut cooled cake and arrange as shown. Frost "cone" with Chocolate frosting, reserving ½ cup. Place writing tip in pastry bag. Fill with remaining ½ cup Chocolate frosting. Pipe waffle pattern onto "cones." Decorate with chocolate sprinkles. Spread Vanilla frosting on "ice cream" parts. Decorate with assorted decors and jelly beans. Top each with maraschino cherry.   *12 to 16 servings*

Tip: Use tip of knife to draw lines in frosting for waffle pattern as guide for piping chocolate frosting.

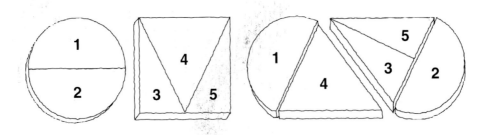

PORCUPINE CUPCAKES

1 package Duncan Hines® Moist Deluxe® Cake Mix (any flavor) 1 container Duncan Hines® Creamy Homestyle Chocolate Frosting	Sliced almonds

1 Preheat oven to 350°F. Place 2½-inch paper liners in 24 muffin cups.

2 Prepare, bake and cool cupcakes following package directions for basic recipe. Frost cupcakes with Chocolate frosting. Place sliced almonds upright on each cupcake to decorate as a "porcupine."

24 cupcakes

Tip: Slivered almonds can be used in place of sliced almonds.

BROWNIE CANDY CUPS

1 package Duncan Hines® Double Fudge Brownie Mix 2 eggs ⅓ cup water	¼ cup Crisco® Vegetable Oil 30 miniature peanut butter cup candies, wrappers removed

1 Preheat oven to 350°F. Place 30 (2-inch) foil liners in muffin pans or on baking sheets.

2 Combine brownie mix, fudge packet from Mix, eggs, water and oil in large bowl. Stir with spoon until well blended, about 50 strokes. Place 2 level measuring tablespoons batter in each foil liner. Bake at 350°F 10 minutes. Remove from oven. Push 1 peanut butter cup candy in center of each cupcake until even with surface of brownie. Bake 5 to 7 minutes longer. Remove to cooling racks. Cool completely.

30 brownie cups

Tip: Pack these brownies in your child's lunch bag for a special treat.

CAPTIVATING CATERPILLAR CUPCAKES

1 package Duncan Hines®
   Moist Deluxe® White
   Cake Mix
3 egg whites
1⅓ cups water
2 tablespoons Crisco®
   Vegetable Oil
½ cup star decors, divided
1 container Duncan
   Hines® Creamy
   Homestyle Vanilla
   Frosting

Green food coloring
6 chocolate sandwich
   cookies, finely
   crushed (see Tip)
½ cup candy-coated
   chocolate pieces
⅓ cup assorted jelly beans
Assorted nonpareil
   decors

1 Preheat oven to 350°F. Place 24 (2½-inch) paper liners in muffin cups.

2 Combine cake mix, egg whites, water and oil in large bowl. Beat at low speed with electric mixer until moistened. Beat at medium speed 2 minutes. Fold in ⅓ cup star decors. Fill paper liners about half full. Bake at 350°F 18 to 23 minutes or until toothpick inserted in center comes out clean. Cool in pans 5 minutes. Remove to cooling racks. Cool completely.

3 Tint Vanilla frosting with green food coloring. Frost one cupcake. Sprinkle ½ teaspoon chocolate cookie crumbs on frosting. Arrange 4 candy-coated chocolate pieces to form caterpillar body. Place jelly bean at one end to form head. Attach remaining star and nonpareil decors with dots of frosting to form eyes. Repeat with remaining cupcakes.

24 cupcakes

Tip: To finely crush chocolate sandwich cookies, place cookies in resealable plastic bag. Remove excess air from bag; seal. Press rolling pin on top of cookies to break into pieces. Continue pressing until evenly crushed.

BACK-TO-SCHOOL PENCIL CAKE

1 package Duncan Hines®
  Moist Deluxe® Cake
  Mix (any flavor)
2 containers Duncan
  Hines® Creamy
  Homestyle Vanilla
  Frosting, divided

Red and yellow food
  coloring
Chocolate sprinkles

1 Preheat oven to 350°F. Grease and flour 13×9×2-inch pan.

2 Prepare, bake and cool cake following package directions for basic recipe.

3 For frosting, tint 1 cup Vanilla frosting pink with red food coloring. Tint remaining frosting with yellow food coloring.

4 To assemble, cut cooled cake and arrange on large baking sheet or piece of sturdy cardboard as shown. Spread pink frosting on cake for eraser at one end and for wood at other end. Spread yellow frosting over remaining cake. Decorate with chocolate sprinkles for pencil tip and eraser band (see Photo). *12 to 16 servings*

Tip: To make this cake even more special, reserve ¼ cup Vanilla frosting before tinting yellow. Place writing tip in decorating bag. Fill with frosting. Pipe name of child, teacher or school on pencil.

CHOCOLATE BUNNY COOKIES

1 package Duncan Hines® Chewy Fudge Brownie Mix (19.8 ounces)	1⅓ cups pecan halves (96) 1 container Duncan Hines® Creamy Homestyle Dark Chocolate Fudge Frosting
1 egg	
¼ cup water	
¼ cup Crisco® Vegetable Oil	Vanilla milk chips

1 Preheat oven to 350°F. Grease baking sheets.

2 Combine brownie mix, egg, water and oil in large bowl. Stir with spoon until well blended, about 50 strokes. Drop by 2 level teaspoonfuls 2 inches apart on greased baking sheets. Place two pecan halves, flat-side up, on each cookie for ears. Bake at 350°F 10 to 12 minutes or until set. Cool 2 minutes on baking sheets. Remove to cooling racks. Cool completely.

3 Spread Dark Chocolate Fudge frosting on one cookie. Place vanilla milk chips, upside down, on frosting for eyes and nose. Dot each eye with frosting using toothpick. Repeat for remaining cookies. Allow frosting to set before storing cookies between layers of waxed paper in airtight container.

4 dozen cookies

Tip: For variety, frost cookies with Duncan Hines® Vanilla Frosting and use semi-sweet chocolate chips for the eyes and noses.

FOOTBALL CAKE

1 package Duncan Hines®
   Moist Deluxe® Devil's
   Food Cake Mix

DECORATOR FROSTING
¾ cup confectioners sugar
2 tablespoons Crisco®
   Shortening
1 tablespoon cold water
1 tablespoon non-dairy
   powdered creamer

¼ teaspoon vanilla extract
Dash salt
1 container Duncan
   Hines® Creamy
   Homestyle Chocolate
   Frosting

1 Preheat oven to 350°F. Grease and flour 10-inch round cake pan. Prepare cake following package directions for basic recipe. Bake at 350°F 45 to 55 minutes or until toothpick inserted in center comes out clean.

2 For decorator frosting, combine confectioners sugar, shortening, water, non-dairy powdered creamer, vanilla extract and salt in small bowl. Beat at medium speed with electric mixer 2 minutes. Add more confectioners sugar to thicken or water to thin frosting as needed.

3 Cut cake and remove 2-inch slice from center. Arrange cake as shown. Spread chocolate frosting on sides and top of cake. Place basketweave tip in pastry bag. Fill with decorator frosting. Make white frosting laces on football.

12 to 16 servings

Tip: If a 10-inch round pan is not available, make 2 football cakes by following package directions for baking with two 9-inch round cake pans.

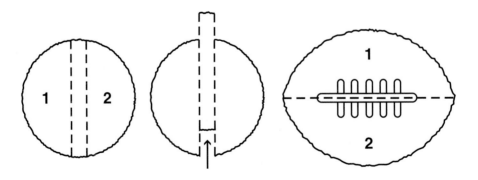

BERRY SURPRISE CUPCAKES

1 package Duncan Hines®
    Moist Deluxe® White
    Cake Mix
3 egg whites
1⅓ cups water
2 tablespoons Crisco®
    Vegetable Oil
3 sheets (0.5 ounce each)
    strawberry chewy
    fruit snacks

1 container Duncan
    Hines® Creamy
    Homestyle Vanilla
    Frosting
2 pouches (0.9 ounce
    each) chewy fruit
    snack shapes, for
    garnish (optional)

1 Preheat oven to 350°F. Place 24 (2½-inch) paper liners in muffin cups.

2 Combine cake mix, egg whites, water and oil in large bowl. Beat at low speed with electric mixer until moistened. Beat at medium speed 2 minutes. Fill each liner half full with batter.

3 Cut three fruit snack sheets into 9 equal pieces. (You will have 3 extra squares.) Place each fruit snack piece on top of batter in each cup. Pour remaining batter equally over each. Bake at 350°F 18 to 23 minutes or until toothpick inserted in center comes out clean. Cool in pans 5 minutes. Remove to cooling racks. Cool completely. Frost cupcakes with Vanilla frosting. Decorate with fruit snack shapes, if desired.

12 to 16 servings

Tip: To make a Berry Surprise Cake, prepare cake following package directions. Pour half the batter into prepared 13×9×2-inch pan. Place 4 fruit snack sheets evenly on top. Pour remaining batter over all. Bake and cool as directed on package. Frost and decorate as described above.

Duncan Hines®

SIMPLE BUT SINFUL DESSERTS

DOUBLE BERRY LAYER CAKE

1 package Duncan Hines®
   Moist Deluxe®
   Strawberry Supreme
   Cake Mix
⅔ cup strawberry jam,
   divided
2½ cups fresh blueberries,
   rinsed, drained and
   divided

1 container (8 ounces)
   frozen whipped
   topping, thawed and
   divided
Fresh strawberry slices,
   for garnish

1 Preheat oven to 350°F. Grease and flour two 9-inch round cake pans.

2 Prepare, bake and cool cake following package directions for basic recipe.

3 Place one cake layer on serving plate. Spread with ⅓ cup strawberry jam. Arrange 1 cup blueberries on jam. Spread half the whipped topping to within ½ inch of cake edge. Place second cake layer on top. Repeat with remaining ⅓ cup strawberry jam, 1 cup blueberries and remaining whipped topping. Garnish with strawberry slices and remaining ½ cup blueberries. Refrigerate until ready to serve.   *12 servings*

Tip: For best results, cut cake with serrated knife; clean knife after each slice.

CHOCOLATE CHERRY TORTE

1 package Duncan Hines® Moist Deluxe® Devil's Food Cake Mix
1 can (21 ounces) cherry pie filling
¼ teaspoon almond extract

1 container (8 ounces) frozen whipped topping, thawed and divided
¼ cup toasted sliced almonds, for garnish (see Tip)

1 Preheat oven to 350°F. Grease and flour two 9-inch round cake pans.

2 Prepare, bake and cool cake following package directions for basic recipe. Combine cherry pie filling and almond extract in small bowl. Stir until blended.

3 To assemble, place one cake layer on serving plate. Spread with 1 cup whipped topping, then half the cherry pie filling mixture. Top with second cake layer. Spread remaining pie filling to within 1½ inches of cake edge. Decorate cake edge with remaining whipped topping. Garnish with sliced almonds.   *12 to 16 servings*

Tip: To toast almonds, spread in a single layer on baking sheet. Bake at 325°F 4 to 6 minutes or until fragrant and golden.

STRAWBERRY CELEBRATION CAKE

1 package Duncan Hines®
   Moist Deluxe®
   Strawberry Supreme
   Cake Mix
1 cup strawberry
   preserves, heated
1 container Duncan
   Hines® Creamy
   Homestyle Cream
   Cheese Frosting

Strawberry halves, for
   garnish
Mint leaves, for garnish

1 Preheat oven to 350°F. Grease and flour 10-inch Bundt® or tube pan.

2 Prepare, bake and cool cake following package directions for basic recipe.

3 Split cake horizontally into three even layers. Place bottom cake layer on serving plate. Spread with ½ cup warm preserves. Repeat layering. Top with remaining cake layer. Frost cake with Cream Cheese frosting. Garnish with strawberry halves and mint leaves. Refrigerate until ready to serve.   *12 to 16 servings*

Tip: For a delicious variation, substitute 1 cup seedless red raspberry jam for the strawberry preserves.

BUTTER PECAN PIE

1 cup coarsely chopped
   pecans
¼ cup butter or margarine
1 container Duncan
   Hines® Creamy
   Homestyle Vanilla
   Buttercream Frosting
1 package (8 ounces)
   cream cheese,
   softened

1 cup frozen non-dairy
   whipped topping,
   thawed
1 prepared 9-inch graham
   cracker crumb pie
   crust
Pecan halves, for
   garnish

1 Place pecans and butter in 10-inch skillet on medium heat. Cook, stirring constantly, until butter is lightly browned. Pour into heat-proof large bowl. Add Vanilla frosting and cream cheese. Stir until thoroughly blended.

2 Fold in whipped topping. Pour into prepared crust. Garnish with pecan halves, if desired. Refrigerate for 4 hours or until firm.   *8 to 10 servings*

HUMMINGBIRD CAKE

1 package Duncan Hines® Moist Deluxe® Yellow Cake Mix	**4 eggs**
1 package (4-serving size) vanilla instant pudding and pie filling mix	**1 teaspoon ground cinnamon**
	½ medium-size ripe banana, cut up
½ cup Crisco® Vegetable Oil	**½ cup finely chopped pecans**
1 can (8 ounces) crushed pineapple, well drained (reserve juice)	**¼ cup chopped maraschino cherries, well drained**
Reserved pineapple juice plus water to equal 1 cup	**Confectioners sugar**

1 Preheat oven to 350°F. Grease and flour 10-inch Bundt® or tube pan.

2 Combine cake mix, pudding mix, oil, pineapple, 1 cup juice and water mixture, eggs and cinnamon in large bowl. Beat at low speed with electric mixer until moistened. Beat at medium speed 2 minutes. Stir in banana, pecans and cherries. Pour into pan. Bake at 350°F 50 to 60 minutes or until toothpick inserted in center comes out clean. Cool in pan 25 minutes. Invert onto serving plate. Sprinkle with confectioners sugar.   *12 to 16 servings*

Tip: Also great with Cream Cheese Glaze. For glaze, heat 1 container Duncan Hines® Creamy Homestyle Cream Cheese frosting in microwave at HIGH (100% power) 30 seconds. Do not overheat. Stir until smooth.

FANTASY ANGEL FOOD CAKE

1 package Duncan Hines® Angel Food Cake Mix Red and green food coloring	1 container Duncan Hines® Creamy Homestyle Cream Cheese Frosting

1 Preheat oven to 350°F.

2 Prepare cake following package directions. Divide batter into thirds and place in 3 different bowls. Add a few drops red food coloring to one. Add a few drops green food coloring to another. Stir each until well blended. Leave the third one plain. Spoon pink batter into ungreased 10-inch tube pan. Cover with white batter and top with green batter. Bake and cool following package directions.

3 To make Cream Cheese glaze, heat frosting in microwave at HIGH (100% power) 20 to 30 seconds. Do not overheat. Stir until smooth. Set aside ¼ cup warm glaze. Spoon remaining glaze on top and sides of cake to completely cover. Divide remaining glaze in half and place in 2 different bowls. Add a few drops red food coloring to one. Add a few drops green food coloring to the other. Stir each until well blended. Using a teaspoon, drizzle green glaze around edge of cake so it will run down sides. Repeat with pink glaze.   *16 servings*

Tip: For marble cake, drop batter by spoonfuls, alternating colors frequently.

PUMPKIN PIE CRUNCH

1 can (16 ounces) solid
  pack pumpkin
1 can (12 ounces)
  evaporated milk
3 eggs
1½ cups sugar
4 teaspoons pumpkin pie
  spice

½ teaspoon salt
1 package Duncan Hines®
  Moist Deluxe® Yellow
  Cake Mix
1 cup chopped pecans
1 cup butter or
  margarine, melted
Whipped topping

1 Preheat oven to 350°F. Grease bottom of 13×9×2-inch pan.

2 Combine pumpkin, evaporated milk, eggs, sugar, pumpkin pie spice and salt in large bowl. Pour into pan. Sprinkle dry cake mix evenly over pumpkin mixture. Top with pecans. Drizzle with melted butter. Bake at 350°F 50 to 55 minutes or until golden. Cool completely. Serve with whipped topping. Refrigerate leftovers. *16 to 20 servings*

Tip: For a richer flavor, try using Duncan Hines® Moist Deluxe® Butter Recipe Golden Cake Mix.

RICH DOUBLE CHOCOLATE CREAM TORTE

BROWNIE
1 package Duncan Hines®
    Milk Chocolate Chunk
    Brownie Mix
3 eggs

⅓ cup water
⅓ cup Crisco® Vegetable
    Oil
½ cup finely chopped nuts

CHOCOLATE BUTTER CREAM
1 package (6 ounces)
    semi-sweet chocolate
    chips, melted
½ cup butter or
    margarine, softened

1 cup whipping cream,
    chilled and divided

WHIPPED CREAM
2 tablespoons sugar
1 tablespoon chocolate
    sprinkles

1 Preheat oven to 350°F. Grease and flour 9-inch round pan.

2 For brownie, combine brownie mix, eggs, water, oil and nuts in large bowl. Stir with spoon until well blended, about 50 strokes. Pour into pan. Bake at 350°F 35 to 40 minutes. Cool 30 minutes. Run knife around edge of pan. Invert onto serving platter. Cool completely.

3 For chocolate butter cream, stir together melted chocolate, butter and 2 tablespoons whipping cream. Spread over top of cooled brownie.

4 For whipped cream, beat remaining whipping cream and sugar in medium bowl with electric mixer on high speed 1 to 3 minutes or until thick. Spread over chocolate butter cream. Sprinkle with chocolate sprinkles. Refrigerate until ready to serve. *8 to 12 servings*

Tip: Chilling the beaters and bowl before whipping the cream decreases whipping time and helps insure good volume.

LUSCIOUS KEY LIME CAKE

CAKE

1 package Duncan Hines®
   Moist Deluxe® Lemon
   Supreme Cake Mix
1 package (4-serving size)
   lemon instant
   pudding and pie
   filling mix

4 eggs
1 cup Crisco® Vegetable
   Oil
¾ cup water
¼ cup Key lime juice
   (see Tip)

GLAZE

2 cups confectioners
   sugar
⅓ cup Key lime juice
2 tablespoons water
2 tablespoons butter or
   margarine, melted

Additional
   confectioners sugar
Lime slices, for garnish
Fresh strawberry slices,
   for garnish (optional)

1 Preheat oven to 350°F. Grease and flour 10-inch Bundt® or tube pan.

2 **For cake,** combine cake mix, pudding mix, eggs, oil, ¾ cup water and ¼ cup Key lime juice in large bowl. Beat at low speed with electric mixer until moistened. Beat at medium speed 2 minutes. Pour into pan. Bake at 350°F 50 to 60 minutes or until toothpick inserted in center comes out clean. Cool in pan 25 minutes. Remove cake from pan onto cooling rack. Return cake to pan. Poke holes in top of warm cake with toothpick or long-tined fork.

3 **For glaze,** combine 2 cups confectioners sugar, ⅓ cup Key lime juice, 2 tablespoons water and melted butter in medium bowl. Pour slowly over top of warm cake. Cool completely. Invert onto serving plate. Dust with additional confectioners sugar. Garnish with lime slices and strawberry slices, if desired.   *12 to 16 servings*

Tip: Fresh or bottled lime juice may be substituted for the Key lime juice.

RICH PUMPKIN CHEESECAKE

CRUST

1 package Duncan Hines®
   Moist Deluxe® Spice
   Cake Mix

½ cup butter or
   margarine, melted

FILLING

3 packages (8 ounces
   each) cream cheese,
   softened
1 can (14 ounces)
   sweetened
   condensed milk

1 can (16 ounces) solid
   pack pumpkin
4 eggs
1 tablespoon pumpkin
   pie spice

TOPPING

1 package (2½ ounces)
   sliced almonds
2 cups whipping cream,
   chilled

¼ cup sugar

1 Preheat oven to 375°F.

2 **For crust,** combine cake mix and melted butter in large bowl; press into bottom of ungreased 10-inch springform pan.

3 **For filling,** combine cream cheese and sweetened condensed milk in large bowl. Beat with electric mixer at high speed 2 minutes. Add pumpkin, eggs and pumpkin pie spice. Beat at high speed 1 minute. Pour over prepared crust in pan. Bake at 375°F 65 to 70 minutes or until set. Cool completely on rack. Refrigerate 2 hours. Loosen cake from sides of pan; remove sides of pan.

4 **For topping,** preheat oven to 300°F. Toast almonds on baking sheet at 300°F 4 to 5 minutes or until fragrant and light golden brown. Cool completely. Beat whipping cream in medium bowl with electric mixer on high speed until soft peaks form. Gradually add sugar; beat until stiff peaks form. Spread over top of chilled cake. Garnish with toasted almonds. Refrigerate until ready to serve. *8 to 12 servings*

Tip: To prepare in 13×9×2-inch pan, bake at 350°F 35 minutes or until set.

TRIPLE CHOCOLATE FANTASY

CAKE

1 package Duncan Hines® Moist Deluxe® Devil's Food Cake Mix

3 eggs

1⅓ cups water

½ cup Crisco® Vegetable Oil

½ cup ground walnuts (see Tip)

CHOCOLATE GLAZE

1 package (12 ounces) semi-sweet chocolate chips

¼ cup plus 2 tablespoons butter or margarine

¼ cup coarsely chopped walnuts

WHITE CHOCOLATE GLAZE

3 ounces white chocolate, coarsely chopped

1 tablespoon Crisco® Shortening

1 Preheat oven to 350°F. Grease and flour 10-inch Bundt® pan.

2 **For cake,** combine cake mix, eggs, water, oil and ground walnuts in large bowl. Beat at low speed with electric mixer until moistened. Beat at medium speed 2 minutes. Pour into pan. Bake at 350°F 45 to 55 minutes or until toothpick inserted in center comes out clean. Cool in pan 25 minutes. Invert onto serving plate. Cool completely.

3 **For chocolate glaze,** combine chocolate chips and butter in small heavy saucepan. Heat on low heat until chips are melted. Stir constantly until shiny and smooth. (Glaze will be very thick.) Spread hot glaze over cooled cake. Sprinkle with coarsely chopped walnuts.

4 **For white chocolate glaze,** combine white chocolate and shortening in another small heavy saucepan. Heat on low heat until melted, stirring constantly. Drizzle hot glaze over top and sides of cake. *12 to 16 servings*

Tip: To grind walnuts, use a food processor fitted with steel blade. Process until fine.